**FRIENDS
OF ACPL**

Far-Fetched Pets

YOUR

PET

ELEPHANT

By Bobbie Hamsa

Illustrations by Tom Dunnington

Consultant:
  John R. Lehnhardt
  Elephant Keeper
  Lincoln Park Zoo, Chicago

 CHILDRENS PRESS, CHICAGO

CAUTION

Far-fetched pets should not be kept in your house or apartment or yard. Don't ask for one for your birthday or Christmas. Go to the zoo or visit the library. There you can learn more about your favorite far-fetched pet.

Library of Congress Cataloging in Publication Data

Hamsa, Bobbie.
    Your pet elephant.

    (Far-fetched pets)
    SUMMARY: Lists the pleasures and problems of having
an elephant as a pet, including his need for about 500
pounds of vegetation a day and his ability to compact
trash or bring in firewood.
    [1. Elephants—Anecdotes, facetiae, satire, etc.]
1. Dunnington, Tom. II. Title. III. Series.
PZ7.H1887Yoe   [E]   79-26412
ISBN 0-516-03353-0

This is an elephant.
An African elephant.
Pretend that he is your pet.

He has tough gray skin with wrinkles
all over it.

Big, floppy ears.

A long trunk with two knobs
(like fingers) on the end.

And tusks as long as your sofa.

What will you name your pet elephant?

CARE AND FEEDING OF YOUR PET

Elephants eat grass, leaves, branches, bark, and hay. About 500 pounds of it a day.

And they drink two bathtubs full of water.

For a treat, give him peanuts or cane sugar, or whole husked coconuts.

Or, ask Mom to cook up some 11 or 12 pound grain balls made of oats and corn.

Elephants actually *like* baths. Your
pet would love to bathe with you, but
your tub is just too small.

Instead, take him outside on nice summer
days and squirt him with the hose.

Or, take him to the river and let him roll in the mud.

Your elephant will need a nice big place to call his own. A garage would be nice. Or maybe your sister's room. Remember though, he snores pretty loudly.

If he's young, your elephant is about the size of a St. Bernard. He won't grow very fast, but by the time you're in high school, he'll be bigger than your dining room.

Think about where you will put your pet elephant.

Show your elephant you love him.
Pet him.

Scratch him behind the ears, on his forehead, and on his back. Pet his tongue.

Then rub his belly with a rock.

Stay away from your elephant's eyes.
And never, never pull his tail—he
really hates that.

Your elephant can't jump, so don't ask him to play leapfrog.

He can't climb something too steep.
So keep him off the roof and out of trees.

19

TRAINING

There are many things your elephant is naturally perfect for.

You can't beat having one under you when there's a parade in town.

Or when you want to see a baseball game today. And lost your allowance yesterday.

Your elephant is very smart. So you
can teach him to do many things.
Pick apples . . .
    mash trash into neat flat bundles . . .
        help you build a tree house . . .
        water Mom's plants . . .
unstick Dad's car when it's stuck in the mud.

Next time you clean your aquarium,
teach him to suck all the water out.
It's much neater that way and he can do
it in a flash. *(Take the fish out first.)*

He'll pick up your blocks in the living room and snort them out in your bedroom when Dad says, "Get those toys out of here!"

He can do simple math problems, and
take you to school and back. (Allow at
least two hours for the trip.)

Teach him to pick up your clothes . . .
bring in firewood . . . and if you have time,
teach him to wipe his feet. Mom will
like that.

These are only a few of the things
your pet can do.

Can you think of more?

If you take good care of him, your
elephant will live maybe 70 years.
And he'll be the best pet you ever had.

Facts about your pet African Elephant (Loxodonta africana)

Size at birth: 3 feet tall at the shoulder, about 150 to 200 pounds

Number of newborn: one, twins on rare occasions

Average size when grown: 10 feet tall at the shoulder, about 5 tons (10,000 pounds)

Type of food eaten: vegetation; grass, leaves, bark, fruit, roots

Expected lifespan: maximum 70 years, normal 45 to 55 years

Names—male: bull
        female: cow
        young: calf
        group: herd

Where found: African continent below the Sahara Desert, but not in the far southern areas.

About the Author

Bobbie Hamsa was born and raised in Nebraska, far away from any far-fetched pets. Mrs. Hamsa has a Bachelor of Arts Degree in English Literature from the University of Nebraska. She is married and has a son, John.

Mrs. Hamsa is an advertising copywriter in Omaha. She writes print, radio, and television copy for a full range of accounts, including Mutual of Omaha's "Wild Kingdom," the five-time Emmy Award winning wild animal series and sometime resource for far-fetched pets.

About the Artist:

Tom Dunnington divides his time between book illustration and wildlife painting. He has done many books for Childrens Press, as well as working on textbooks, and is a regular contributor to "Highlights for Children." Tom lives in Oak Park, Illinois.